# The
# QUESTIONS
## *and*
# ANSWERS

---

**BE READY FOR
LIFE'S CHALLENGES.**

*Protect your most valuable assets:*
*Your life, health, home, business, and auto*

---

## *on*
# INSURANCE
# PLANNER

## TONY STEUER, CLU, LA, CPFFE, INSURANCE LITERACY ADVOCATE

LIFE INSURANCE
SAGE PRESS

This publication is designed to provide accurate and authoritative information in regard to the subject matter covered. It is sold with the understanding that the publisher and author are not engaged in rendering legal, accounting, or other professional services. If legal advice or other expert assistance is required, the services of a competent professional should be sought.

Published by Life Insurance Sage Press
Alameda, CA

Copyright ©2014 Tony Steuer

Distributed by River Grove Books

For ordering information or special discounts for bulk purchases, please contact River Grove Books at PO Box 91869, Austin, TX  78709, 512.891.6100.

Design and composition by Stacey Meinzen
Cover design by Stacey Meinzen
Interior Images courtesy © 2014 Microsoft Corporation. All rights reserved

Publisher's Cataloging-In-Publication Data

Steuer, Anthony.
   The questions and answers on insurance planner : be ready for life's challenges / Tony Steuer, CLU, LA, CPFFE.—First edition.

   pages : illustrations ;  cm

   Issued also as an ebook.
   ISBN: 978-0-9845081-6-7

   1. Insurance—United States. 2. Insurance, Life—United States. 3. Homeowners' insurance—United States. 4. Insurance, Automobile—United States. I. Title.

HG8531 .S74 2014
368/.973                                                                      2014944453

First Edition

Other Edition(s):
eBook ISBN: 978-0-9845081-7-4

# The Questions and Answers on Insurance Planner

The Questions and Answers on Insurance Planner is designed to help you understand what insurance you do and do not need, along with buying and monitoring tips. Take the time to investigate your options and to make sure you have full protection at the lowest cost.  This planner will help you buy the right kind and amount of insurance for your needs and make sure your current policies are sufficient.

## Using this Planner:

This planner provides you with information, tips, and tools on the most common types of insurance coverage.  It will assist you in understanding your insurance needs, obtaining insurance, and monitoring and using it when needed.  Insurance is complex and this planner provides you with simple answers.

If you are faced with a devastating loss of life, health, income, home, or auto, having the right insurance in place can make a huge difference.  Take control by educating yourself and using that knowledge to obtain the appropriate insurance and to save on your insurance premiums.

# Questions and Answers on Life Insurance

**What's the Bottom Line on Life Insurance?**

The purpose of life insurance is to replace income for someone who is dependent upon the insured's income – nothing more, nothing less. The type of life insurance you need depends on the length of time for which you need it. Most people have a set period of time for which they need life insurance – perhaps 30 years to protect a mortgage, 18 years to provide for a child, etc. As their assets grow (retirement accounts, etc.), their need for life insurance will decline. There are two types of life insurance:

*Term Insurance:* Pays a death benefit when someone dies. Provides coverage for a limited time period and does not accrue a cash value.

*Permanent Life Insurance:* Pays a death benefit, can be continued for a longer period of time/full lifetime, planned level premium, may accumulate a cash value. Sold under many different names: Whole Life, Universal Life, Variable Life, Universal life, indexed life.

**How Much Life Insurance Do You Need?**

The most commonly mentioned method of calculating life insurance needs is the simple rule of thumb of using a multiple of your income (anywhere from 6 to 15 times). While rules of thumb may be helpful, they do not take each individual's situation into consideration.

If you know the amount of income that needs to be replaced (assuming that this a permanent level income), you can perform a reverse calculation by dividing the income stream needed by a conservative, reasonable rate of return if you were to invest the entire proceeds and leave the principal intact (such as a 5% annual rate of return). For example, if your need is for an annual before tax income stream of $50,000 then divide by 5% ($50,000/.05) resulting in a death benefit of $1,000,000.

> **TIPS:** A spouse/domestic partner who does not have earnings (or lower earnings) still contributes economic value and may have a life insurance need. Also, do not forget to name a contingent beneficiary. If a contingent beneficiary is not named, the life insurance proceeds would become part of the insured's estate.

**Things to consider when buying life insurance:** The main factors that will impact your premium classification are: Height & Weight (BMI), Tobacco Usage (what type & frequency), Family Health History, Driving History, Blood Pressure, Cholesterol, Cholesterol/HDL ratio, Alcohol/Substance abuse and Hazardous Activities & Occupations. After that the companies will look closely at any and all medical conditions that would impact your life expectancy such as heart disease and cancer. Criteria will vary from company to company.

Visit the resource center @ www.tonysteuer.com for tools to determine how much you need today. Keep in mind that you should only buy as much life insurance as you currently need rather than what you might need in the future. Also, as you accumulate other assets, your need for life insurance will usually decline.

## How Do I Monitor It?

Life insurance doesn't end at purchase. Policies are living things and there are many components that can affect their performance. This is particularly true with **permanent** policies that build cash value over time. For example, if you've taken out **policy loans** or have a **Universal/Variable/Equity Indexed, etc.** policy — which requires vigilant attention to **premium** payments and the investment portfolio — you'll want to be aware of how much money it'll take to keep those policies **in-force**, and whether you can afford to *keep* them **in-force**.

**Term Insurance:** If your term policy is more than a couple of years old and your health is good, then you should consider looking at current available options, as term rates may have decreased. Know when your guaranteed premium ends and also know the last date to convert your policy to permanent insurance. Check the marketplace — use an advisor or online website with access to multiple companies.

**Permanent Insurance:** To begin the monitoring process, get in touch with your life insurance carrier and request a current in-force illustration. You can download a sample in-force illustration request letter at www.tonysteuer.com. An in-force illustration projects future performance of a life insurance using current values rather than the projections at the time of the policy issue. Permanent life insurance policies are made up various components that impact policy performance, including earnings (interest rates/dividend rates, etc), mortality costs, cost of insurance charges, and expense charge. In-force illustrations are critical and the ONLY WAY to find out if your life insurance policy is performing as expected. An in-force illustration will help you answer the following questions:

- Is the policy fully funded? In other words, will it continue to maturity (maximum age) with current premiums based on current assumptions?
- If the policy is not fully funded, what is the premium required to fund the policy to maturity, based on current assumptions?
- Is the policy overfunded? Have you paid in more than required?
- Can you terminate premiums and still have the policy continue to maturity based on current assumptions?

If your policy is not performing as expected, it can be due to one or more of the following: lower than expected earnings (interest rate, dividends, etc.), higher than expected mortality costs or cost of insurance and/or higher than projected expense charges. For more information, read: *"Why Would My Life Insurance Policy Underperform"* at www.tonysteuer.com/resources.

By understanding, maintaining, and monitoring your policy, you will avoid any unpleasant surprises in the future and ensure that the right policy will be there for you when you need it.

THE DANGERS OF POLICY LOANS: Policy loans can be a useful short-term option when immediate cash is needed, but they are not the long-term solution so widely proclaimed. In fact, policy loans (available with most, but not all, forms of permanent life insurance) are one of the most complex, misunderstood, and misused components of a life insurance policy. Out-of-control policy loans can erode a life insurance policy over time, eventually draining the death benefit — and saddling you with a substantial tax bill. Borrowing from a policy can be helpful when times are tough, but loans must be used responsibly. The policy can lapse if the loan is not repaid, and the loans can be complex and destructive if not handled with care. For more details, download the article: The Pitfalls of Policy Loans at www.tonysteuer.com/media

# Questions and Answers on **Disability Insurance**

## What's the Bottom Line on Disability Insurance?

If you are dependent upon your earned income you need disability income insurance. **The odds of a disability are high.** At age 40, the chances of a disability lasting 90 days or more is 21%. The majority of contracts are unaffected by Social Security which requires 12 months of total disability is very stringent in qualification. Coverage can also be used to fund buy-sell agreements, key-person indemnification and business overhead expenses. **The older you get, the higher your chances of being disabled for longer periods of time.**

### Your Chances of Becoming Disabled For More Than 90 Days Before The Age of 65

| AGE | PERCENTAGE DISABLED | ODDS OF BECOMING DISABLED |
|-----|---------------------|---------------------------|
| 25  | 52%                 | 1 out of 2                |
| 30  | 51%                 | 1 out of 2                |
| 35  | 48%                 | 4 out of 9                |
| 40  | 45%                 | 4 out of 9                |
| 45  | 40%                 | 2 out of 5                |
| 50  | 34%                 | 1 out of 3                |
| 55  | 16%                 | 1 out of 6                |

**Social Security Disability Income Insurance (SSDI):** The Social Security Administration (SSA) provides long-term disability benefits based on your salary and the number of years you have worked and contributed to the Social Security system. Social Security replaces only a limited portion of your salary, and the qualifications to receive benefits are very strict. To learn more about SSDI and to read Social Security's fact sheets and actuarial publications, go to www.ssa.gov/disability

**Employer/Group Long Term Disability Insurance:** Your employer will provide a basic coverage amount and you may be automatically enrolled or you will be given the option to join at your employer's open enrollment period. Employers will sometimes offer the option of paying on a pre-tax or post-tax basis. If you pay on a pre-tax basis, your benefits will be subject to income tax. If you pay on an after-tax basis, your benefits will not be subject to income tax. Some employers will also allow you to purchase additional coverage. Keep in mind that this coverage is typically not portable and you can typically only get it without a medical exam when you're first offered the coverage. Even if you have group long-term disability, your coverage is most likely less than you think it is. A supplemental policy can provide you with a significant amount of additional coverage. The majority of group plans pay a pre-tax benefit, which means any benefits are subject to income tax, there is usually a maximum monthly benefit, and bonuses and commissions are typically not covered.

**TIP:** If you have group disability coverage here's how to calculate your current coverage and how much additional individual disability insurance coverage may be available to you:
(Current Annual Gross Income) times (% covered). 50-60 is the norm. Most plans have a maximum benefit cap, so use that if applicable. Then subtract your gross income tax rate (35-40%) for your current after-tax long-term disability benefit. An individual disability program will usually replace about 70%+ of your after-tax income.

**How Do I Buy Disability Insurance?**

Every disability insurance policy has certain core parameters that can differ from company to company.

- **Benefit amount:** This is the maximum monthly benefit for your policy. The worksheet and information above will help you determine your need.
- **Occupation (disability) definition:** The disability definition is the most important part of the policy because everything else stems from it. Some policies pay benefits only if you are unable to perform the duties of any occupation for which you are reasonably qualified by training, experience, and education. However, depending on the definition of disability, the own occupation rider is usually not necessary and can significantly add to your premium.
- **Elimination period**: This is the number of days that you must pay for covered services before the insurance company will make payments (also known as a waiting period and comparable to a deductible)
- **Benefit period**: This is the length of time for which your benefit will be paid.  This is usually a set number of years (example: 5 years) or to age X (such as to age 65).  Most policies do allow a policy holder to continue the coverage past age 65 with a decreased benefit period of 1 or 2 years.
- **Riders**: Non-Cancelable (guarantees against future premium increases), residual or partial disability rider, extended/transition benefit, lost income provision, cost of living adjustment, future increase option, catastrophic disability benefit rider, and supplemental social insurance rider.

> **TIP: Most policies are guaranteed renewable.  This is very important.**  "Guaranteed Renewable" guarantees that the insurer cannot terminate the policy as long as the premiums are paid, and the insured doesn't have to reapply at any point to continue coverage.   Premiums cannot be raised based on an individual's circumstances, however they can be increased for an entire class of policyholders.  No other aspect of the policy can be changed.

**How Do I Monitor It?** Life changes so it's important to monitor your policy to make sure that it still fits your current situation, especially if you've had a change in income or employment. A few things to lookout for include:

- Exclusions – sometimes a disability policy is issued with an exclusion for a certain illness or injury.  The exclusion can be removed after a certain period.  For example, if you have knee surgery, the insurance company may exclude any disabilities related to the knee for a certain period of time.  However, the insurance companies will not usually remove this automatically.  You will need to request to have this exclusion removed.
- Change in employer – have you gained or lost your Group Long Term Disability Coverage or is it the same?
- Change in income level – has your income increased or decreased?  Your Disability Benefit should be adjusted accordingly either by increasing coverage or decreasing coverage.
- Future purchase option or future increase options – do you have these?  When is it available and are you eligible?  Know the terms and make sure to take advantage if you are eligible.  The insurance companies will typically notify you, although there is no guarantee that they will.

# Questions and Answers on **Long Term Care Insurance**

**What's the Bottom Line on Long Term Care Insurance?** Long Term Care insurance coverage pays for expenses that are not covered by health insurance and/or Medicare.

**Long Term Care Facts:**

- 50% of all Americans age 65 and older will require some type of long term care assistance (California Partnership for Long Term Care Comprehensive Brochure, August 2004)
- Nursing home care is expensive: The 2010 average daily rate in the U.S. for a private room in a nursing home was $206 ($75,190 annually) and a semi-private room is $185 a day (Genworth Financial 2010 Cost of Care Survey)
- During the last 20 years nursing home rates increased at an average rate of over 5% per year and are likely to increase at the same rate.
- 35% of people who enter a nursing facility stay between 1 and 5 years (National Center for Policy Analysis, "A long-term solution to a medicaid problem," 11/17/1995: 2004 National Nursing Home Survey)
- 21% of people in nursing facilities remain for more than 5 years (California Partnership for Long Term Care, 2005).
- The average length of time spent in a nursing home is 2.4 years (MetLife Market Survey of Nursing Home and Assisted Living Cost, 10/2007)

**How Much Long Term Care Insurance Do I Need?**

The amount of long term care insurance you will need depends on whether or not you can go without insurance (self-insure) as well as how much the daily cost of care will be where you live. Take a look at what you may need, what you have in other assets and balance it with a premium that you can afford (even if increased by 25%).

**What about Medicare?**

Medicare only pays for skilled care in a nursing facility for a short period – no longer than 100 days – and only if the patient meets all of Medicare's requirements for receiving daily skilled care. Medicare does not cover long-term custodial care or in-home care.

> **TIP:** Determine if the policy pays on an indemnity basis (a specified amount to the policyholder up to a daily maximum or monthly maximum regardless of the actual cost of care). Example: If $150 in daily medical charges is incurred and the policy has a $200 daily payout, the insured can use the extra $50 for any qualifying expenses.

Every Long Term Care insurance policy has certain core definitions and parameters that can differ from company to company. Long Term Care policies allow you to customize the various components to fit your needs and budget.  It's important to understand each of these components and if it fits your financial plan. These components can vary in definition from company to company. When comparison-shopping, the components should be the same for getting as close as possible to an "apples to apples" comparison.

- **Maximum daily (or monthly) benefit**: This is the maximum specified dollar amount that will be paid on a daily basis for services covered under a policy.   Research facilities and services in the area you plan to live during retirement to find out the current daily cost of care.
- **Elimination period**: This is the number of days that you must pay for covered services before the insurance company will make payments (also known as a waiting period and comparable to a deductible).  Policies can have different definitions for elimination period.
- **Benefit period**: This is the number of days for which benefits will be paid.  Most current policies allow you to carry over unused benefits.  For example, if you are using half of your daily maximum benefit, your benefit period would be twice as long.
- **Inflation rider:** An inflation rider increases your benefit to keep pace with inflationary increases in the cost of long-term care.  Typically options are none, 5% simple and 5% compound.
- **Other riders**: Other riders include assisted living benefits, survivorship benefits, restoration of benefits and non-forfeiture benefits.

**Discounts: Always ask what discounts are available.**  Common discounts are for Preferred Health & Marital/Couples Discount. Companies will usually offer a discount to married couples, couples that share a child, and domestic partners.

**How Do I Monitor Long Term Care Insurance?**  Find out the types of care that are covered under your policy. Many older long term-care policies did not pay for any type of home care or relatively newer types of care like adult day care.

**What If You Receive A Premium Increase?  Consider Your Options:**

1. Do Nothing - keep everything as is and pay the new premium.  Can you afford this new premium? Are the benefits that you will receive still worth the premium?
2. Adjust different components of the policy to reduce the premium.  Ask yourself if you can make the following changes to the policy and still have the coverage remain worthwhile to you:

   a. Reduce the daily benefit amount
   b. Increase the waiting period
   c. Shorten the benefit period
   d. Change your inflation rider – if you have a compound inflation rider, can you change a simple inflation rider?  Can you reduce the inflation rider percentage (for example, from 5% to 4%)?
   e. Change/remove other riders?

3. If your policy has a contingent, non-forfeiture benefit, consider taking it if you cannot afford the premiums (this would provide a paid-up reduced pool of benefits).
4. Cancel the policy

# Questions and Answers on Health Insurance:

## What's the Bottom Line on Health Insurance?

Health insurance will give you access to medical care and preventative care. When purchasing health insurance, your choices typically will fall into one of three categories:

**Traditional** fee-for-service health insurance plans are usually the most expensive choice, but they offer you the most flexibility in choosing health care providers.

**Health maintenance organizations (HMOs)** offer lower co-payments and cover the costs of more preventive care, but your choice of health care providers is limited. The National Committee for Quality Assurance evaluates and accredits HMOs. You can find out whether one is accredited in your state by calling 1-888-275-7585. You can also get this information, as well as report cards on HMOs, by visiting www.ncqa.org.

**Preferred provider organizations (PPOs)** offer lower co-payments like HMOs, but give you more flexibility in selecting a provider. A PPO gives you a list of providers you can choose from.

WARNING: If you go outside the HMO or PPO network of providers, you may have to pay a portion or all of the cost.

When choosing among different health care plans, you'll need to read the fine print and ask lots of questions, such as:

- Do I have the right to go to any doctor, hospital, clinic, or pharmacy I choose?
- Are specialists such as eye doctors and dentists covered?
- Does the plan cover special conditions or treatments such as pregnancy, psychiatric care, and physical therapy?
- Does the plan cover home care or nursing home care?
- Will the plan cover all medications my physician may prescribe?
- What are the deductibles? Are there any co-payments?
- What is the most I will have to pay out of my own pocket to cover expenses?
- If there is a dispute about a bill or service, how is it handled? In some plans, you may be required to have a third party settle the claim.

## Group Policies

Many consumers have health care coverage from their employers. Others have medical care paid through a government program such as Medicare, Medicaid, or the Veterans Health Administration.   If you have lost your group coverage from an employer as the result of unemployment, death, divorce, or loss of "dependent child" status, you may be able to continue your coverage temporarily under the ***Consolidated Omnibus Budget Reconciliation Act (COBRA).*** You pay for this coverage. When one of these events occurs, you must be given at least 60 days to decide whether you wish to purchase the coverage.

**Medicare and Medicaid**

There are also health insurance programs for people who are seniors, disabled, or have low incomes.
- **Medicaid** provides health insurance for people with low incomes, children, and pregnant women. Eligibility is determined by your state.
- **Medicare** provides health insurance for people who are 65 years or older, some younger people with disabilities, and those with kidney failure.

Contact the Centers for Medicare & Medicaid Services for more information on benefits. Most states also offer free or low-cost coverage for children who do not have health insurance. Visit www.insurekidsnow.gov or call 1-877-KIDS-NOW (543-7669) for more information.

**Affordable Care Act**

The 2010 Affordable Care Act (ACA) puts in place comprehensive health insurance reforms that will roll out over several years. Most provisions will take effect by 2014; a timeline is available at healthcare.gov/law/timeline.

The law is intended to lower health care costs, provide more health care choices, and enhance the quality of health care for all Americans. Major provisions affecting consumers include:

- Coverage for seniors who hit the Medicare Prescription Drug "donut hole," including a rebate for those who reach the gap in drug coverage.
- Expanded coverage for young adults, allowing them to stay on their parents' plan until they are 26 years old.
- Providing access to insurance for uninsured Americans with pre-existing conditions.
- Expanded preventive care (for example, wellness visits and mammograms) to Medicare and Medicaid participants.
- Medical coverage to children not eligible for care under Medicaid.

For more information about the law as well as basic information about health insurance, go to www.healthcare.gov.

# Questions and Answers on Annuities

**What's the Bottom Line on Annuities?**

An annuity is a contract between you and an insurance company that requires the insurer to make payments to you, either immediately or in the future. You buy an annuity by making either a single payment or a series of payments. Similarly, your payout may come either as one lump-sum payment or as a series of payments over time.

Annuities are helpful if you have a specific need that cannot be fulfilled through another investment product. The most common reason to use annuities is for periodic payments for a specified amount of time (this can be for the rest of your life, or the life of your spouse or another person or for a set number of years). Annuities are a good solution for someone who has issues with spending their savings. Purchasing an annuity will "lock" up their money and allow them to receive a guaranteed income. When you compare an annuity to other investments, you will find higher fees and you will surrender charges that over the long run will cost you more and result in lower accumulated funds.

DANGER: A common selling point is that annuities usually feature tax-deferred growth on the income and investment gains until money is withdrawn. That's true under current tax law. However, current tax law is not guaranteed and if the law is changed, there will be no recourse for annuity owners. Purchasing any type of financial product solely for tax reasons usually is not recommended.

If you feel that an annuity is the right investment choice for you, you can purchase them either as an immediate annuity – where the annuitant receives benefits immediately – or as a deferred annuity – where the benefits are deferred until a later date.

**Annuity Phases:**

There are two phases for annuities:

1. **Accumulation phase**: When your payments are made into the annuity and accumulate based on the type of annuity.

2. **Payout phase:** When you receive your payments back, along with any investment income and gains. You may take the payout in one lump-sum payment, or you may choose to receive a regular stream of payments, generally monthly. Annuity payments are based on a percentage/ratio calculation of premiums paid compared to gains. In other words, if you paid in $50,000 and your earnings were $50,000, your ratio would be 50%, which would be subject to ordinary income tax. Please note that this does not constitute tax advice and we are not tax advisors.

**Basic Types of Annuities:**

- **Fixed annuity:** The insurance company promises you a minimum rate of interest and a fixed amount of periodic payments. State insurance commissioners regulate fixed annuities. Please check with your State's Department of Insurance website (links to each State's DOI can be found at www.naic.org) about the risks and benefits of fixed annuities and to confirm that your insurance broker is registered to sell insurance in your state.

- **Variable annuity:** The insurance company allows you to direct your annuity payments to different investment options (usually mutual funds). Your payout will vary depending on how much you put in, the rate of return on your investments, and expenses. The SEC regulates variable annuities. Variable annuities include several charges such as mortality & expense risk charge, administrative fees, underlying fund expenses, and fees and charges for other features, penalties, surrender charges, and partial withdrawal limitations.

- **Indexed annuity:** This annuity combines features of securities and insurance products. The insurance company credits you with a return that is based on a stock market index, such as the Standard & Poor's 500 Index. State Insurance Commissioners regulate Indexed annuities. Indexed annuities have several limitations and fees such as administrative fees, fees and charges for other features, surrender charges, partial withdrawal limitations, interest (earnings) cap, and participation rate.

Variable annuities and indexed annuities are very complex financial products. If you do decide to opt for either of these products, make sure that you fully understand all the risks and fees that are involved. These annuities carry investment risk.

Note that if you sell or withdraw money from a variable annuity too soon after your purchase, the insurance company will impose a "surrender charge." This is a type of sales charge that applies in the "surrender period," typically six to eight years after you buy the annuity. Surrender charges will reduce the value of – and the return on – your investment.

**DANGER**: Realize that if you are investing in an annuity through a tax-advantaged retirement plan, such as a 401(k) plan or an Individual Retirement Account (IRA), you will get no additional tax advantages from a variable annuity. In such cases, consider buying the annuity only if it makes sense because of the annuity's other features.

**How Do I Monitor an Annuity?**

Review the above information in this section and decide whether you really need to maintain the annuity. If you do not need to maintain it, determine your options to terminate it (if you can terminate it). If you do wish to maintain the annuity, compare to other annuities for performance and contract terms along with reviewing the company's financial strength.

# Questions and Answers on Auto Insurance

**What's the Bottom Line on Auto Insurance?**

Auto Insurance is required by most states. Check with your state's Department
of Insurance to find out if your state requires coverage and if so, at what amount. If you have a car loan,
your lender will also have minimum coverage standards. If your state does not require auto insurance,
you still should consider the coverage, as the cost of not having the coverage can be very high.
Visit: www.tonysteuer.com/l-i-regulatory-links/ to locate your state's Department of Insurance website and
contact information.

**Required Coverage (by State Insurance Departments):**
- **Bodily injury liability:** This is usually described in three numbers, which refer to limits for the different
types of liability coverage. These coverage limits are the most your insurance policy will pay for (1)
injuries to any one person, (2) all persons injured in an accident, and (3) property damage.
- **Property damage liability:** This coverage pays for damages you cause to someone else's car or to
objects and structures your car hits.

**Coverage that May Be Required in Your State:**
- **Uninsured and underinsured motorist coverage:** Uninsured motorist coverage reimburses you if an
uninsured or a hit-and-run driver hits you. Underinsured motorist coverage pays when an at-fault
driver doesn't have enough insurance to fully pay for your loss.
- **Medical payments or personal injury protection (PIP):** Uninsured motorist coverage reimburses you if
an uninsured or a hit-and-run driver hits you. Underinsured motorist coverage pays when an at-fault
driver doesn't have enough insurance to fully pay for your loss.

**Coverage Required by a Lender:**
While the following coverage is typically required when receiving an auto loan, it is also a good idea for most
drivers who do not have any auto loan debt.

- **Collision:** This coverage pays for damage to your car from a collision with another car, an object or
pothole, or from flipping over, etc.
- **Comprehensive:** This coverage reimburses you for damage to your car that's not caused by a collision.
This includes theft, hail, windstorm, flood, fire and hitting animals. Comprehensive coverage also will
reimburse you if your windshield is pitted, cracked or damaged. Some companies won't charge you a
deductible for windshield repairs.
- **No-fault:** If you live in a no-fault state, your own insurance company pays for injuries to you and your
passengers regardless of who's at fault. Most no-fault states also let you sue the at-fault driver if you
have serious injuries. However, you still must file a claim with the at-fault driver's insurance company
to be paid for damage to your vehicle.

**Premiums:**
Each insurance company uses their own method to calculate their premium. Premiums range on a number of
key factors listed below. Insurance companies offer a range of discounts, so be sure to get multiple quotes
from quality insurance companies (see choosing an insurance company on page 16).

Key factors affecting premiums include:

- Driving records (from the last 3 - 5 years)
- Age, Gender, and Marital Status
- Type of vehicle
- Where you live
- Vehicle use (annual mileage)
- Prior insurance coverage

- Previous claims
- Limits chosen for liability coverage
- Deductibles chosen for comprehensive and collision coverage
- Credit scores (some states ban credit scores as a factor to determine premiums)

Strategies and/or criteria for receiving discounts include:

- Bundling policies (buying multiple policies from one company)
- Putting multiple vehicles under one policy
- Having airbags
- Having anti-theft devices

- Taking a defensive driver course
- Driving safely
- Being an age deemed less risky (over 21)
- Finding association or group discounts

## ALWAYS ASK WHAT DISCOUNTS ARE AVAILABLE

**TIP:** Make sure you have enough coverage to meet your needs. Do not just buy the minimum legally required limits for Uninsured/Underinsured Motorist and Bodily Injury & Personal Injury Protection. If affordability is an issue, consider dropping comprehensive coverage and raising your deductible before dropping any essential coverage.

### How To Monitor Your Policy:

When you receive your car insurance policy renewal, do not sign it until you've taken these steps:

1. **Check for changes.** Compare the policy renewal language with your existing policy to catch any changes in coverage or price. If there are changes, call your insurer to find out why.
2. **Re-evaluate your needs.** If you are driving fewer miles per week than you had been, you might be eligible for a lower insurance rate. Likewise, if you have an older car, you may decide you can do without optional collision coverage. You may be paying more than your car is worth. Examples of circumstance changes that may change your auto insurance premiums include a switch to working from home (rather than at an office) and having children that reach driving age (teenagers are much more expensive than adults).
3. **Compare providers.** In addition to getting a quote from your current insurance provider, seek quotes online or by phone from several competitors.
4. **Choose the policy that offers the best value.** Do not focus on price alone, but on the amount of coverage offered for that price. Compare items such as deductibles, exclusions, and coverage limits.
5. **Raise the deductible on collision and comprehensive coverages.** If you have an old car with a low cash value, you might want to drop these coverages altogether.
6. **Make sure your information is accurate and up-to-date.** Your car insurance company will determine your rates based on factors such as your age, driving record, credit history, and location. You may be eligible for a lower rate if you have recently modified your driving habits.

# Questions and Answers on Homeowners Insurance:

## What's the bottom line on Homeowner's Insurance?

Homeowners insurance pays claims for damages to your home, garage, and other outbuildings, as well as for loss of furniture and other personal property due to damage or theft (both at home and away from home). In addition, homeowners insurance pays for additional living expenses if you rent temporary quarters while your house is being repaired.

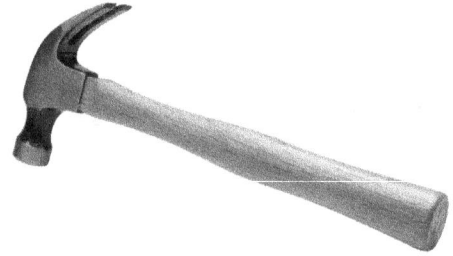

## What is Covered?

- Most homeowners policies will not protect you from a flood, a hurricane, or an earthquake loss. You may be able to purchase these coverages by adding an earthquake or flood endorsement to your insurance policy, or through the National Flood Insurance Program (NFIP).
- Homeowners insurance also includes liability for bodily injury and property damage that you may cause to others through negligence, and for accidents happening in and around your home, as well as away from home, for which you are responsible.
- Homeowners insurance also pays for any injuries occurring in and around your home to anyone other than you or your family. Medical payments coverage also pays claims for injuries outside your home that you, a family member living with you, or your pet cause.
- Homeowners policies generally provide limited coverage for money, gold, jewelry, and stamp and coin collections.

**TIP:** Ask about exclusions. Many property policies on the market today exclude (will not pay for) certain types of damage. Ask the insurer, agent or broker exactly what causes of loss and what items are **NOT** covered. If you want full coverage, make that clear to the insurance company in writing. **Ask whether the policy excludes or limits coverage for damage due to water, earthquakes, earth movement, mold, construction defects, or other common perils. Keep good notes in a safe place.**

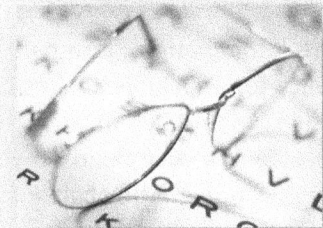

## Umbrella Policies:

You can add more personal liability with a standalone "umbrella" policy. This is a cost-effective way to increase your liability coverage by $1 million or more, in case you are at fault in an accident or someone is injured on your property. It supplements the insurance you already have for home, auto, and other personal property.

For assistance in deciding how much insurance coverage to buy, view information about saving money on homeowners and renters insurance.

## How Do I Monitor My Homeowner's Insurance?

**TIP:** Raising your deductible is the best way of keeping your premium affordable without reducing your protection.

- **Consider a higher deductible.** Increasing your deductible by just a few hundred dollars can make a big difference in your premium.

- **Ask your insurance agent about discounts.** You may be able to get a lower premium if your home has safety features such as dead-bolt locks, smoke detectors, an alarm system, storm shutters or fire retardant roofing material. Persons over 55 years of age or long-term customers may also be offered discounts.

- **Insure your house, NOT the land under it.** After a disaster, the land is still there. If you do not subtract the value of the land when deciding how much homeowner's insurance to buy, you will pay more than you should.

- **Act now.** Do not wait till you have a loss to find out if you have the right type and amount of insurance.

- **Get replacement coverage, not an "actual cash value" policy.** Make certain you purchase enough coverage to replace what is insured. This will give you the money to rebuild your home and replace its contents. An "Actual Cash Value" policy is cheaper but pays only what your property is worth at the time of loss your cost minus depreciation for age and wear.

- **Ask about special coverage you might need.** You may have to pay extra for computers, cameras, jewelry, art, antiques, musical instruments, stamp collections, etc.

- **Remember that flood and earthquake damage are not covered by a standard homeowners policy.** The cost of a separate earthquake policy will depend on the likelihood of earthquakes in your area.

- Homeowners who live in areas prone to flooding should take advantage of the National Flood Insurance Program.

- **If you are a renter, do not assume your landlord carries insurance on your personal belongings.** Purchase a separate policy for renters.

For more information on homeowners insurance in your state, contact your state insurance regulator. You may be able to save hundreds of dollars a year on homeowners' insurance by shopping around.

# Questions & Answers on Choosing an Insurance Company

**What's the Bottom Line on Choosing an Insurance Company?**

The financial strength of an insurance company is highly important because an insurance policy is a long-term commitment.   This strength can be determined by looking at rating agency assessments of the companies you are considering.

**Rating Agencies**

Rating agencies evaluate insurance companies by examining their financial condition and operating performance, using specific criteria. The ratings agencies assign ratings of a company's financial strength and ability to meet obligations to policyholders. Insurance Companies are rated by these third party agencies on a regular basis and offer their ratings and analysis online for free.  However, some insurance companies are not rated by all of the rating services.

There are four main rating agencies, and each agency's rating system varies in its stringency and its methodology.  All four agencies consider a company's financial leverage, management stability, recent performance, overall financial health, and external factors such as competition, diversification, and market presence.

Here are the websites for the top four rating agencies:

- AM Best: www.ambest.com
- Fitch: www.fitchratings.com
- Moody's: www.moodys.com
- Standard & Poor's: www.standardandpoors.com

A rule of thumb is simply to identify the top-rated companies that offer the particular type of policy you desire.  Do not worry too much about the details.  An insurance company with a top rating from at least three of the four agencies is in great standing.

**Other Considerations:**

1. **Does the insurance company hold itself to any official ethical standards?** Each carrier adheres both to its own ethical practices and to basic guidelines dictated by each state's respective insurance department. (You can find a directory of each state's insurance department at www.naic.org.)

2. **How many complaints – and of what nature – are filed against the company in question?**  Most insurance carriers aren't going to have a spotless record, but some will be worse than others.  Each state's department of insurance maintains data on the number of complaints filed against an insurance company, as well as pending class-action lawsuits. To find your state's department of insurance, go to the website of the National Association of Insurance Commissioners (NAIC) at www.naic.org. Then run an online search for the company's name to see if any negative comments exist on unofficial complaint sites.

# Questions and Answers on Choosing an Insurance Agent

## What's the Bottom Line on Choosing An Agent?

Insurance is complex and it is often worth paying an experienced professional a reasonable commission and/or fee to find you the right policy and company to suit your specific needs. Working with a qualified insurance adviser will help you to get an objective opinion and weed through the options best for you. However, if you are comfortable with your understanding of your needs and the products available, going to a website that offers comparisons can work for you. Keep in mind that companies offer the same premium no matter how you buy the policy – through an agent, a website, etc.

The advisers you choose from should represent multiple companies. If they represent only one company they can offer you only that company's products—not necessarily the best products in the marketplace.

The policy you buy through an agent or broker will include a commission based on the total premium for the policy. Do not be shy about asking questions to make sure the commission and/or fee you will be charged isn't out of line. Beware of paying both a fee and commission where it's not necessary. You can negotiate fees and on certain insurance products, commissions can be negotiated.

REMEMBER: Being educated will help you to get the right insurance for you. You are in charge and it's your money, so say no if what you are offered is not just right for you.

## State Insurance Department Compliance

Any person selling insurance must be licensed. As with an attorney needing to pass the bar in any state in which he/she intends to practice, life insurance salespeople are required to pass an exam administered by each state's department of insurance, as well as to enroll in continuing education seminars on a regular basis. *The representative you ultimately select must be licensed in the state where you, the insured, either work or live.* You can find a directory of these departments on www.naic.org.com. The resources and compliance standards within state insurance departments may be more lax in some states than in others. On most state insurance departments' websites you can research whether an insurance representative is licensed.

## What Do All Those Professional Designations Mean?

Life insurance agents may earn such professional designations as Chartered Life Underwriter (CLU) and Life Underwriter Training Council Fellow (LUTCF). Agents who are also financial planners may carry such credentials as Chartered Financial Consultant (ChFC), Certified Financial Planner (CFP), or Personal Financial Specialist (CPA–PF). These designations indicate that the agent has completed advanced training, passed rigorous exams, and is serious about professional development. CLU is the only designation that specifically focuses strictly on life insurance and is by far the most comprehensive in the life insurance arena. A Chartered Property Casualty Underwriter (CPCU) can assist you with homeowners and auto insurance and related areas.

# Your Coverage: Policy Tracker

| Insurance Type | Company | Policy # | Issue Date | Premium | Agent Name | Agent Contact # | Agent Email | Last Reviewed Date |
|---|---|---|---|---|---|---|---|---|
| Home | | | | | | | | |
| Flood | | | | | | | | |
| Earthquake | | | | | | | | |
| Umbrella | | | | | | | | |
| Auto | | | | | | | | |

| Life Insurance | |
|---|---|
| Company | |
| Policy # | |
| Issue Date | |
| Premium | |
| Agent Name | |
| Agent Contact # | |
| Agent Email | |
| Last Reviewed Date | |
| Death Benefit Type of Contract | |

| Disability Insurance | |
|---|---|
| Company | |
| Policy # | |
| Issue Date | |
| Premium | |
| Agent Name | |
| Agent Contact # | |
| Agent Email | |
| Last Reviewed Date | |
| Monthly Benefit | |
| Waiting Period | |
| Benefit Period | |

| Medical/Vision/Dental Insurance | |
|---|---|
| Company | |
| Policy # | |
| Issue Date | |
| Premium | |
| Agent Name | |
| Agent Contact # | |
| Agent Email | |
| Last Reviewed Date | |
| Deductible | |
| Co-Insurance/Co-Pay | |

| Long Term Care Insurance | |
|---|---|
| Company | |
| Policy # | |
| Issue Date | |
| Premium | |
| Agent Name | |
| Agent Contact # | |
| Agent Email | |
| Last Reviewed Date | |
| Daily Benefit | |
| Benefit Period | |

# Important Insurance Terms:

**Actual Cash Value (ACV):** The "old" price of an item as it was pre-loss, sometimes explained as the price a willing buyer would have paid for that item immediately before it was damaged or destroyed.

**Beneficiary:** The person named in the policy to receive the insurance proceeds at the death of the insured. A secondary or contingent beneficiary will receive the proceeds if the primary beneficiary cannot collect.

**Benefit:** The amount payable by the insurance company to a claimant, assignee, or beneficiary under each coverage.

**Claim:** A request for payment of a loss, which may come under the terms of an insurance contract.

**Contestable Period:** A period of time (usually the first 2 years of a policy) during which the insurance company can revoke your policy.

**Commission:** The part of an insurance premium paid by the insurer to an agent or broker for his services in procuring and servicing the insurance.

**Declarations Page:** Usually the first or second page of the policy. States the name and address of the insured location, policy number, dollar amounts of coverages, mortgage company (additional named insured), endorsements, and riders.

**Death Benefit:** A payment made to a designated beneficiary upon the death of the insured.

**Deductible:** The amount you have to pay out-of-pocket on a claim before the policy pays the loss. Higher policy deductibles mean lower policy premiums.

**Dividend:** A policyholder's share in the insurer's divisible surplus fund apportioned for distribution, which may take the form of a refund of part of the premium on a participating policy.

**Endorsement:** An add-ons or change to the basic policy that changes the terms, conditions, or limits of coverage. Also known as a "rider".

**Issue Date:** The date your policy became effective and was issued by the insurance company.

**Policy Loan:** A loans taken out against the account.

**Premium:** The amount paid to an insurer or reinsurer in consideration of his acceptance of a risk.

**Premium Mode:** Frequency of the premium payment (monthly, quarterly, etc.).

**Replacement Coverage (RC):** The "new" price of what it would cost to actually repair or replace a damaged or destroyed item.

**Rider:** An optional addition to the primary policy (to insure a child, for example).

**Surrender Charge:** The charge for early surrender of a policy. This is the difference between the accumulation (or account) value and the net cash surrender value. The surrender charge typically decreases each year and disappears after a certain number of years.

## Miscellaneous Insurance Types:

**Accidental Death and Dismemberment:** A type of coverage that pays benefits, sometimes including reimbursement for loss of income, in case of sickness, accidental injury, or accidental death.

**Burial insurance:** A type of life insurance which is paid out upon death to cover final expenses, such as the cost of a funeral.

**Catastrophic Health Care Insurance:** A health plan that only covers certain types of expensive care, like hospitalizations.

**Credit insurance:** Repays some or all of a loan when certain circumstances arise to the borrower such as unemployment, disability, or death.

**Critical illness insurance**: Provides a lump sum cash payment if the policyholder is diagnosed with one of the critical illnesses listed in the insurance policy.

**Dental insurance:** Designed to pay a portion of the costs associated with dental care.

**Directors and officers liability insurance (D&O):** Protects an organization (usually a corporation) from costs associated with litigation resulting from errors made by directors and officers for which they are liable.

**Errors and omissions insurance (E&O):** Business liability insurance for professionals such as insurance agents, real estate agents and brokers, architects, third-party administrators (TPAs) and other business professionals.

**Earthquake insurance:** A form of property insurance that pays the policyholder in the event of an earthquake that causes damage to the property. Most ordinary home insurance policies do not cover earthquake damage.

**Flood insurance:** Protects against property loss due to flooding. Many U.S. insurers do not provide flood insurance in some parts of the country. In response to this, the federal government created the National Flood Insurance Program which serves as the insurer of last resort.

**General Liability Insurance:** Protects you from damage done to someone else's property by your operations, as well as injuries sustained at your place of business.

**Identity Theft Insurance:** Provides reimbursement to crime victims for the cost of restoring their identity and repairing credit reports. Some companies now include this as part of their homeowners insurance policy; others sell it as a standalone policy. Ask your homeowner policy company for information.

**International Health Care Insurance.** A policy that provides health coverage no matter where you are in the world. The policy term is flexible, so you can purchase it only for the time you will be out of the country.

**Mortgage insurance:** Insures the lender against default by the borrower.

## Miscellaneous Insurance Types Continued:

**Pet insurance:** insures pets against accidents and illnesses; some companies cover routine/wellness care and burial, as well.

**Professional liability insurance:** protects insured professionals against potential negligence claims made by their patients/clients.

**Reinsurance:** A type of insurance purchased by insurance companies or self-insured employers to protect against unexpected losses

**Title insurance:** Provides a guarantee that title to real property is vested in the purchaser and/or mortgagee, free and clear of liens or encumbrances. It is usually issued in conjunction with a search of the public records performed at the time of a real estate transaction

**Travel Insurance:** insurance coverage taken by those who travel abroad, which covers certain losses such as medical expenses, loss of personal belongings, travel delay, and personal liabilities.

**Workers Compensation Insurance:** insurance covers your employees if they have an accident on the job site, paying for everything from medical costs to time off to costs associated with any continued injury.

**There are many other types of insurance available for just about anything that you can think of:**

Alien abduction insurance, All-Risk Insurance, Assumption reinsurance, Aviation insurance, Bancassurance, Bloodstock Insurance, Bond insurance, Builder's risk insurance, Business interruption insurance, business overhead expense disability insurance, Business owner's policy, Casualty insurance, Catastrophe bond, Chargeback insurance, Collateral protection insurance (CPI), Computer insurance, Contents insurance, Credit insurance, Crime insurance, Death bond, Deposit insurance, Defense Base Act (DBA) Insurance, Directors and officers liability insurance, Divorce Insurance, Dual trigger insurance, Environmental liability insurance, Expatriate insurance, Fidelity bond, Financial reinsurance, Fraternal Insurance, GAP Insurance, General insurance, Guaranteed asset protection insurance, Income protection insurance, Inland marine insurance, Interest rate insurance, Key person insurance, Kidnap and ransom insurance, Landlords' insurance, Legal expenses insurance, Lenders mortgage insurance, Liability insurance, Livestock Insurance, Longevity bond, Longevity insurance, Marine insurance, Media Liability insurance, Mortgage insurance, Mutual insurance, No-fault insurance, Nuclear Incident Insurance, Parametric Insurance, Payment Protection Insurance, Pension Term Assurance, Perpetual Insurance, Pet Insurance, Political Risk Insurance, Pollution Insurance, Prize Indemnity Insurance, Product Liability, Professional Liability Insurance, Property insurance, Protection and Indemnity Insurance, Purchase Insurance, Reinsurance, Rent Guarantee Insurance, Retrospectively Rated Insurance, Satellite insurance, Savings Deposit Insurance, Shipping Insurance, Social Insurance, Terminal Illness Insurance, Terrorism Insurance, Trade Credit Insurance, Travel Insurance, Tuition Insurance, Uninsured Employer, Vehicle insurance, Volcano Insurance, Wage insurance, War Risk Insurance, Weather Insurance, Windstorm Insurance, Zombie Fund

# A Note from the Author

Dear Reader,

Thank you for checking out *The Questions and Answers on Insurance Planner*. I hope that you feel in control and empowered with your money.

Healthy money habits help you understand all areas of your financial life and how they fit together. Being able to ask the right questions will bring you success in meeting your goals and understanding how everything fits together.

If you loved the book and have a minute to spare, I would really appreciate a short review on your favorite book site. You're the reason why I continue to write about changing the way we think about money through financial preparedness and advocating for integrity in financial services.

If you think this book might help a family member or friend with their own money, feel free to invite them to join the Get Ready Movement at www.tonysteuer.com. They'll receive the Get Ready Roadmap as well as helpful tips for reviewing all aspects of their money.

So what's next? Join the Get Ready Movement and stay up to date on the latest in changing the way we think about money by subscribing to the Get Ready! Newsletter and joining our community.

Cheers,

Tony

P.S. Listen to *The Get Ready Money Podcast*: Change the way you think about money. It includes insightful conversations with thought leaders that will provide you with practical advice that demystifies the complexities of finance and helps you build healthy habits that actually work.

P.S.S. If you are passionate about helping people feel empowered with their money, then please join the Get Ready! Expert Money Guides: Dedicated to Helping People Change the Way They Think about Money group on LinkedIn.